STAR SCENE CONFIDENTIAL

What's Hot, WHAT'S HOT?

Ashley Tisdale

Rihanna

Jonas Brothers

By Michael-Anne Johns

SCHOLASTIC INC.

New York   Toronto   London   Auckland   Sydney
Mexico City   New Delhi   Hong Kong   Buenos Aires

Cover Front: Miley Cyrus: © Sara De Boer/Retna Ltd.; Zac Efron: © Lionel Hahn/Abaca USA/Newscom; Demi Lavato: © Andrew H. Walker/Getty Images; **Cover Back:** Rihanna: © Walik Goshorn/Retna Ltd.; Ashley Tisdale: © Dan Kulu/Vanit.de/ Retna Ltd; Selena Gomez: © Frederick M. Brown/Getty Images
Page 1: (left to right) © Adam Orchon/Everett Collection; © Neil King/eyevine/ZUMA Press; © Aude Guerrucci/AFP/Getty Images; **Page 4:** (top left) Noel Vasquez/Getty Images; (middle) Arshamian/Laguna Images/ZUMA Press; (bottom left) Sharkpixs/ZUMA Press; (bottom right) Splash News/Newscom; **Page 4-5:** (top) Frank Micelotta/Getty Images; (bottom) George Napolitano/FilmMagic/Getty Images; **Page 5:** (bottom right) John Parra/WireImage/Getty Images; (top right) Douglas C. Pizac/AP Photo; **Page 6:** David Longendyke/Everett Collection; **Page 7:** (top) Chris Polk/WireImage/ Getty Images; **Page 8:** (top) Frank Micelotta/WireImage/Getty Images; (bottom left) Patrick Rideaux/Rex USA; (bottom) Patrick Rideaux/Rex USA; **Page 9:** (left to right) Zuma/Newscom; Evan Agostini/AP Photo; **Page 10:** (top) Miguel Garcia/ WireImage/Getty Images; (bottom) David Atlas/Retna Ltd.; **Page 11:** Kevin Winter/Getty Images; **Page 12:** Jon Kopaloff/ FilmMagic/Getty Images; **Page 13:** (top) INF Photo/Newscom; (bottom) Jason Winslow / Splash News/Newscom; **Page 14:** (top) Sara De Boer / Retna Ltd; (bottom) Tom Meinelt/Pacific Photos/Newscom; **Page 15:** (top) Mark Sullivan/WireImage/Getty Images; (bottom) Henry S. Dziekan III/Retna Ltd.; **Page 16:** (top) Andrew Marks/Retna Ltd.; (bottom) Whittle/ Splash News/Newscom; **Page 17:** (top) Mark Sullivan/WireImage/Getty Images; (bottom) Paul Fenton/ZUMA Press; **Page 18:** Andrew H. Walker/Getty Images; **Page 19:** (top) Andrew H. Walker/Getty Images; (bottom) Jean-Paul Aussenard/ WireImage/Getty Images; **Page 20:** (top) Reinhold Matay/AP Photo; (inset) RD/Dziekan/Retna Digital; (bottom) Dimitrios Kambouris/WireImage/Getty Images; **Page 21:** Mark Davis/Getty Images; **Page 22:** (top) Lionel Hahn/Abaca USA/News-com; (bottom) Andreas Branch/PatrickMcMullan.com/Sipa Press/Newscom; **Page 23:** (top) Dan Gorder/FilmMagic/Getty Images; (middle) Steve C. Wilson/AP Photo; (bottom) Splash News/Newscom; **Page 24:** (top right) Miguel Perez/Retna Ltd.; (top left) Kevin Mazur/WireImage/Getty Images; (bottom right) Theo Wargo/WireImage/Getty Images; (bottom left) Jeff Daly/Getty Images; **Page 25:** (top) Sara De Boer/Retna Ltd; (middle) WENN Photos/Newscom; (bottom left) Kelly A. Swift/Retna Ltd; (bottom right) RD/Smith/Retna Digital; **Page 26:** Jason Merritt/FilmMagic/Getty Images; **Page 27:** (top) Theo Wargo/WireImage/Getty Images; (bottom) Jeff Vespa/WireImage/Getty Images; **Page 28:** (top) Jeffrey Mayer/WireI-mage/Getty Images; (bottom) Andrew Gombert/epa/Corbis; **Page 29:** (top) Prince Williams/FilmMagic/Getty Images; (bottom) Michael Loccisano/FilmMagic/Getty Images; **Page 30:** Sara De Boer/Retna Ltd; **Page 31:** Baxter/Abaca USA/ Newscom; **Page 32:** Matt Sayles/AP Photo; **Page 33:** (left) All Access/Rex USA; (right) Zandy Mangold/Animal Fair Media/ Getty Images; **Page 34:** (top) INF Photo/Newscom; (bottom) Johns Pk/Splash News/Newscom; **Page 35:** AJ Sokalner/ AcePictures/Newscom; **Page 36:** Mark Von Holden/WireImage/Getty Images; **Page 37:** (top left) Chris Ashford/Camera Press/Retna Ltd; (bottom left) Jason Kempin/FilmMagic/Getty Images; (bottom right) Andrew Marks/Retna Ltd; (top right) Chris Ashford/Camera Press/Retna Ltd; **Page 38:** (top) Neil King/eyevine/ZUMA Press; (bottom) Tina Paul/Camera Press/ Retna Ltd; **Page 39:** Rena Durham/Retna Ltd.; **Page 40:** (top) Michael Bezjian/WireImage/Getty Images; (bottom) Bruce Glikas/FilmMagic/Getty Images; **Page 41:** Adriana M. Barraza/LOLWENN Photos/Newscom; **Page 42:** Ursula Dueren/dpa/ Corbis; **Page 43:** Armando Gallo/Retna Ltd; **Page 44:** (top) Carrie Devorah/WENN Photos/Newscom; (bottom left) Sara De Boer/Retna Ltd; (bottom middle) Michael Buckner/Getty Images; (bottom right) Jennifer Cooper/Corbis; **Page 45:** (top) Jamie McCarthy/WireImage/Getty Images; (middle) Matt Sayles/AP Photo; (bottom) Matt Sayles/AP Photo; **Page 46:** (left) Frank Micelotta/Getty Images for Fox; (right) Tony Barson/WireImage/Getty Images; **Page 47:** (top) Evan Agostini/ AP Photo; (bottom) Kevin Mazur/WireImage/Getty Images; **Page 48:** (top) Don Arnold/WireImage/Getty Images; (bottom) Frank Micelotta/Getty Images

ISBN-10: 0-545-07690-0

ISBN-13: 978-0-545-07690-6

© Scholastic, 2009
Published by Scholastic Inc.

SCHOLASTIC and associated logos are trademarks and/or registered trademarks of Scholastic Inc.

12 11 10 9 8 7 6 5 4 3 2 1

9 10 11 12/0

Designed by Deena Fleming
Printed in the U.S.A.
First printing, January 2009

CONTENTS

INTRODUCTION

Welcome to pages and pages of fun, fun, fun! In this exciting book, today's hottest stars share their fashion and beauty picks. And even though Zac, Vanessa, Miley, the Jo-Bros, and the rest may show up on the mega-money lists in Hollywood, Star Scene Confidential discovered that they are more often just like the rest of us. They love bargains. They know how to shop and save money. You are just as likely to find them in Target or The Gap as at an exclusive designer shop.

On the following pages are great photos of your faves wearing their best-loved outfits as they hang out with their friends, go shopping, or run into a grocery store. Guess what . . . they are just like you! And they have great tips for their fans.

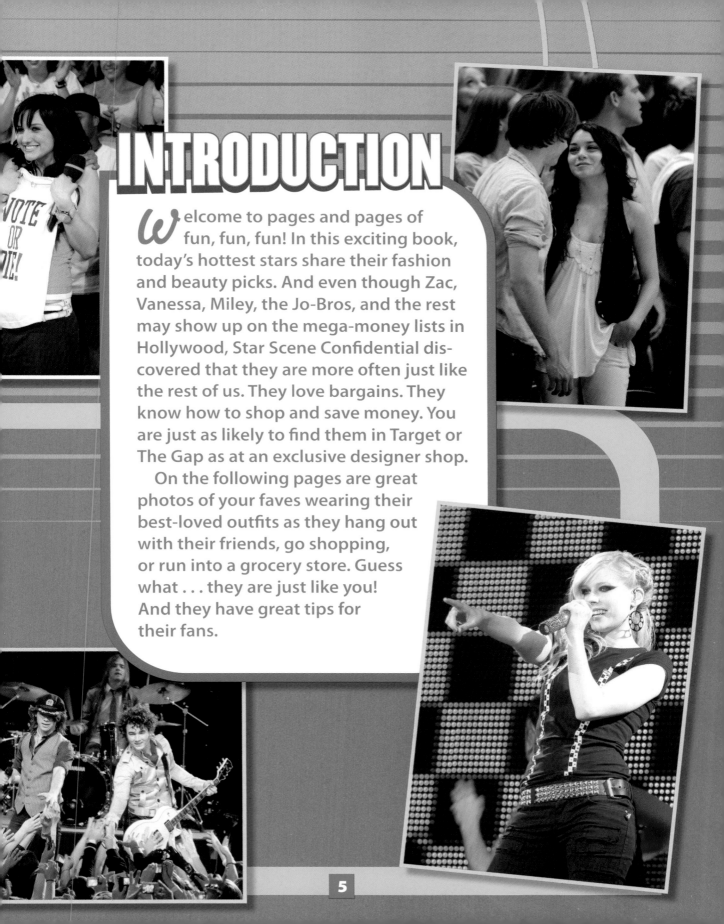

MUST-SEE **MILEY CYRUS** *Stylin*

$\mathscr{M}$iss Miley has become a style icon —mainly because what Miley wears is what her fans wear. Whether it's a boho babydoll top or cowboy boots, Miley insists that her most important style rule is that she is "comfortable."

"My style is really just whatever I'm feeling that day," she says. "Sometimes it's basketball shorts, and now I'm totally into sweats. . . . Sometimes I'll be punky—the next day, I'll be preppy . . . [I] love a cute T-shirt, paired with jeans and tennis shoes. I like to keep it simple but cute; something you're not afraid to get dirty in, but still look pulled together."

Onstage Style

In her everyday life, Miley goes for the comfy and casual outfit. But that changes when she's in front of the camera as Hannah Montana or on a concert stage. That's when the glitter and glam comes out of the closet. Leather, sparkly jackets, sequined tops, skinny jeans, platform shoes—it's bling all the way. A teen magazine fashion editor describes it as a "total pop star" look and probably "trend overload." But the editor continues, "It's appropriate for her character and for being a pop star. . . . It's very trendy, it's very colorful."

The Hannah Montana look is so popular, it actually became a fashion line several years ago. Shortly after the clothing hit the stores, Miley encountered her TV namesake outfits in Nashville. "I went to Macy's and tried on all the Hannah Montana stuff. Then I said, 'This is weird. I'm wearing my face!'"

The RED Carpet

With the mega-popularity of *Hannah Montana*, her sold-out concert tours, her platinum CDs, and her much-anticipated *The Hannah Montana Movie*, things have changed a bit for Miley. She isn't spending as much time riding horses back home in Nashville as she used to, and her jeans and boots aren't daily-wear anymore. Instead, you'll often find Miley at red-carpet events, where she's decked out in glittery designer dresses and shoes. Well, Miley admits there's a small problem there. "I'm holding my shoes in most pictures you see of me at red-carpet events," she giggles. "If I could go to premieres in my sweats, I would!"

Miley's Fun Fashion Tips

"If you wear baggy things and just put a little T-shirt with it, you'll look cute. A girl's outfit doesn't have to be, you know, everything all out there."

"If you stand up straight and look confident, that's the best way to make your clothes not look so wrinkly or like it's been in the suitcase forever."

"I think natural-looking makeup is the best thing. I always like to wear makeup that's as natural as can be. It's too over-the-top when you start caking makeup on. Don't do it!"

"If you're not comfortable in something, don't wear it—you'll be self-conscious. Just be natural, be yourself, and be confident."

"The best accessory is a smile. A smile makes you look energetic, confident, and alive."

"If I can get it cheaper, then I will!"

MILEY'S MUST HAVES

1. Jeans! Though she likes Juicy Couture, she says most of her jeans are bargains from H&M or The Gap.

2. Lip gloss—"I love making my lips all glossy!"

3. Hats—cowboy to fedora

4. Bracelets—leather bands, charm bracelets, bangles, whatever!

5. Tube socks—"Everyone's like, 'What's with those socks?' But that's my style.

6. Skinny jeans

7. Peace-symbol T-shirts

8. White or brightly colored frame sunglasses

9. Boots—especially cowboy boots

"Miley is a style chameleon. She can change her character at any time. If she's feeling like a rocker chick, she's going to wear a vest and boots over her jeans. The next day, if she wants to look like a classy lady, she's going to flip to the premiere dress. She likes taking risks."

—Tara Swennen, Miley's stylist.

Musical Closets

ASHLEY, VANESSA, MONIQUE, KAYCEE
PEEK INTO THEIR CLOSETS

*T*he teen queens of the *High School Musical* movies, Ashley Tisdale, Vanessa Hudgens, Monique Coleman, and Kaycee Stroh, have also become style icons. The four *HSM* buds are all self-admitted fashion-funsters, but each has a unique look and sense of design that fits their lifestyle, body-shape, and taste. As a matter of fact, the four of them are a perfect portfolio of girls everywhere, proving that anyone can look fabulous!

*L*et's take a minute and check out what their personal choices are when it comes to fashion!

ASHLEY

Fave Dress Style
"Babydoll dresses are always easy—you can make them casual or dressy with whatever shoes you wear."

Fave Overall Style
"I can totally go from vintage-looking one day to very chic the next. I'm always changing it up."

Fave Shoes
"I love flats—I'm more comfortable in them."

Fave Shirt Style
"I have almost every single white shirt from Hollister and Abercrombie. They are the cutest, and they always look polished."

Fave Relaxation Style
"I love sweats. I'd wear them all the time if I could!"

Fave Splurge
"Purses and sunglasses are my favorite splurges."

Fave Style Icon
Gwen Stefani

Fave Stores
★ Hollister
★ Abercrombie & Fitch
★ Wet Seal
★ Kitson
★ V
★ Forever 21

Fave Shopping Advice
"I really like the end-of-the-month sale where everything's marked down."

"I don't go right to the expensive stuff. Anything can look good—it's just how you put it together."

Vanessa Hudgens

Fave Personal Style

♥ "I used to be more conservative. Now my look is more sophisticated."

♥ "For an event, I'll plan my entire look ahead of time. If I feel totally rockin', I'll wear heavy eye makeup and messy hair. But if I want to feel elegant, I'll wear pink makeup and my hair either curly or straight."

♥ "I take any excuse to dress up — I like to wear what feels good."

Fave Fashion Sense

"I love people who like taking chances with fashion."

Fave Fashion/Makeup Advice

"I've learned that bright red lipstick is not the best thing to wear during the day! That was my 'oops' moment."

Fave Stores & Clothing Lines

★ Guess?
★ Miss Sixty
★ Red Ecko
★ Free People

Fave Style Icon

"I love Victoria Beckham. I think she's amazing. She always looks so stylish."

Fave Movie Wardrobe

"HSM, of course! ... The wardrobe department is incredible, but I handpicked which outfit I wore for each scene, and also I picked my accessories. Like for 'All For One,' I picked the red-and-white polka dot outfit—it reminded me of the wildcat spirit. I tried to wear a headband in as many scenes as I could since I wore a lot of them in the first movie."

Fave Article of Clothing

"A vintage '70s jumper."

Fave Relaxation

"I totally want to throw a spa party. Just pampering for all my friends—manicures, pedicures, chilling out. But I'd invite Chris Brown to sing at my party."

Fave Hair Advice

"When I was growing up, there was a time when my hair would break off, and it was really short. The kids used to call me Baldie-Locks! It was horrible, but you learn that things like that [aren't] a big deal. You just shake them off and keep moving."

Fave Fitness Advice

Since Monique recently lost 15 pounds with a healthy diet and exercise plan, she says she always goes to the gym and does Pilates, spinning, weight training, and dance classes. "Whenever I book a hotel now, I make sure it has a gym."

Kaycee Stroh

Fave Accessory

"Shoes! I love shoes!"

Fave Style Icon

"Audrey Hepburn. She's so classy . . . I love the big hat and big glasses. Big is better!"

Fave From Size 20~to~14 Advice

"I don't want people to think that I'm giving in to the pressures of Hollywood—I truly believe that [pretty] doesn't have a waist size. I just want to be healthier and happier."

Fave Stores/ Clothing Line

♥ Torrid: Kaycee models for Torrid and explains why she chose to work with them—"I love that I can go in and know I can find something cute and young. Every time I had an event, I used to dread it. I remember going to department stores with my mom, and she said, 'Look, I'm sorry, but once you're a size 18, it's old lady clothes.' I remember trying stuff on in the dressing room and, at one point, sitting down and crying. I love that [Torrid is] teaching young girls to embrace themselves and they don't have to wear too tight or too baggy clothes that hide their curves."

Monique Coleman

Kaycee Stroh

17

DEMI LOVATO'S FASHION Q&A

*D*isney's newest diva, 16-year-old Demi Lovato of *Camp Rock* and *Princess Protection Program* fame, has become a real force in Hollywood. She acts; she sings; she dances; she plays the guitar, drums, and piano . . . and she's become 'tween and teen girls' fashion role model! The Dallas, Texas, native giggles with her best friend, Selena Gomez, over that last fact. "I never imagined that," Demi says.

*F*or an up-close-and-personal look at Demi's fashion taste, check out this Q&A. . . .

Q: What is your very favorite outfit?
A: Sweat pants, hat, scarf, and Converse sneakers.

Q: What is your favorite item of clothing?
A: Probably jackets!

Q: Describe your fashion style.

A: I'm just me. My style changes, but not drastically. I like to wear what I want to wear. . . . My style is my own—crazy, rockish, and fun!

Q: What stores do you run to when you go to the mall?

A: Forever 21, H&M, Hot Topic, and Aldo for shoes.

Q: Do you ever shop for clothes online?

A: Yes, but when there is no time to go to the store. I'm not a huge fan because you can't try on clothes, and it always seems to take forever to get it.

Q: What's your ultimate beauty tip?

A: I don't like getting bags under my eyes, so I drink lots of water and get plenty of sleep.

EYE GUYS STYLE GUIDE
ZAC, JONAS BROTHERS, CHRIS

Who are your favorite cuties? No question about it—Zac Efron, Nick, Kevin, and Joe Jonas, and Chris Brown! These guys are the dream dates of girls from NYC to Los Angeles, from Chicago to Miami . . . and all points in between. Of course, what really makes them so interesting is that they are talented, down-to-earth, the boys-next-door, and are BF or BFF material. But they also look yummy! So let's check out what they like when it comes to style.

Zacalicious!

From *High School Musical* to *Seventeen Again* to his every-day style, Zac has become a teen trendsetter.

Hairspray Harry!

When Zac changed his hairstyle to his tousled-messy look, a lot of Hollywood sigh guys followed suit. Check out *Gossip Girl's* Chace Crawford and Fall Out Boy's Pete Wentz, and you'll think you fell through the Zac Efron looking glass! The shaggy style has been dubbed by some, "Bowl with Bangs" cut—and can be seen in any school and mall across the country!

White-Out!

Zac's favorite article of clothing is a white T-shirt. He's been known to buy 20 at a time! Of course, he also buys his T-shirts and jeans at thrift stores too—"I can get, like, eight pairs of $3 jeans. Who cares if they don't fit? I can give them back to Goodwill."

The Toes Know
"I have pretty good [feet]. I wear sandals every day."

Fashion No-No

The wardrobe and hairstyle from *Hairspray*—"The weird sweaters were so itchy! They put this stuff in my hair that turned it into a rock. I had to run hot water over it for five minutes to loosen it!"

Fave Clothing Stores
Surprise, surprise—Goodwill and The Gap.

"It" Boy
"It's interesting being in that position, but it's a blast. Just the idea that even one girl has my poster on her wall is kinda crazy. I'm still getting used to it."

411 On the Jo-Bros
Fashion Statements

The brothers from New Jersey are known far and wide for their music and their style!

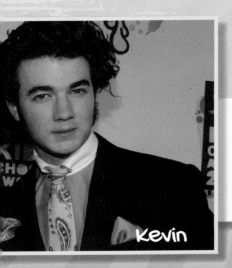

Kevin

- ⭐ "I pay attention to clothing and stuff like that."
- ⭐ Kevin's style has often been described as "Victorian."
- ⭐ Kevin loves shiny shoes—"It's become like a thing."
- ⭐ Kevin goes for bandanas—especially on a bad hair day!

Joe

- ⭐ Joe's become part of the fashion-forward boys club who sport ascots. He looks dapper!
- ⭐ Joe has a collection of sunglasses—it may not rival Elton John's, but he's working on it!
- ⭐ Joe's style is a combo—"'60s, '70s, '80s, '90s—I incorporate everything."
- ⭐ Joe loves his socks—and gets annoyed when Nick goes in and borrows some!

Nick

- ⭐ Nick's favorite headgear is his true-blue Yankee baseball cap.
- ⭐ Nick calls his on-stage style "formal rock," and the final touch is to always roll up his sleeves.
- ⭐ Nick's off-stage style can be described as "almost preppy." He admits, "I like getting dressed up."

Cool Chris

Chris admits that when he was just a little shorty, he loved the hip-hop kid duo Kris Kross—even their style of wearing their clothes backwards. But that was then . . . this is now

Besides his caps and array of logo T-shirts, a Chris Brown must-have is a black or brown leather jacket.

Chris loves hoodies—he's got a whole drawer full of his favorites.

Chris used to be known for his low-slung baggy jeans/T-shirt/kicks look—now he's added designer suits to his closet!

The LRG urban clothing line is one of Chris's favorites.

"I've always got something colorful on," says Chris.

Chris rarely takes off his large diamond stud earrings. "They're me!" he laughs.

Chris has become so known for his "Right Now" look, he even co-hosted the BET fashion special Rip the Runway.

FASHION *Passion*

Check out your faves' must-haves and occasional fashion faux pas!

Miranda Cosgrove *(iCarly)*

Flower hair clips—"They're fun to wear!"

Sophia Bush *(One Tree Hill)*

Ordering e-tail—"I'm a big fan of ordering online from ShopBop and Revolve. You have every color and cut [of jeans] right at your fingertips."

Dress-up vs. casual—"It's great to get done up in a dress, but I don't want to feel like I have to be frilly every day. Sometimes you need to indulge your rock side . . . especially skinny jeans."

Anna Maria Perez de Tagle *(Camp Rock)*

Stores & More—"The first store I head to is Miss Sixty, just because the style is amazing. The second store would have to be Betsey Johnson. I love her dresses. . . . My mom always kind of influenced me on style and fashion."

A.J. Michalka (The Lovely Bones)

Bling, Boots, 'n' Bands!—"I like lots of jewelry. . . .
I wear electrical tape as bracelets. And I like boots. . . . I
think you can dress really simple and have cute accessories,
like a hairband. I always have fun cutting up things that
are out of style and wearing things like belts or vests over
T-shirts."

Aly Michalka (Will)

Just Jeans—"J Brand jeans are my favorite
because they fit really well and are great to wear
on stage. [It took] years of trying on different
pairs of jeans and figuring out what [I] feel best
in. [Go] for jeans that don't get ruined. Quality is
really important. You can still get cheap jeans that
last for ages. . . . There are certain body types
that look good in high-waisted pants . . . like if
you're tall with long legs, it really works. A
boot-cut leg works on any body type."

Meaghan Martin (Camp Rock)

One-Stop-Shopping—"I go to Urban Outfitters, especially for
shoes or dresses."

Jennette McCurdy (iCarly)

Accessorize—"Jewelry can really make a difference in an
outfit. Just get some inexpensive pieces from the mall. It makes
such a difference, because it can make any shirt pop."

Kiely Williams (Cheetah Girls)

Your Own Style—"If you don't have much money or time,
get one really cool signature piece, like a cool tank top or awesome shoes
that you can create your outfit around. It'll draw attention to you."

Brittany Snow *(Hairspray)*

Boot Babe—"I'm liking rain boots right now. I bought two pairs even though it never rains in L.A. I'm obsessed with collecting boots."

Hilary Duff *(Food Fight!)*

T-Girl—"I love Target. You can get everything there—from DVDs to cosmetics, clothes to groceries. My mom bought my new stereo system at Target, and I always pick up video games to take with me when I'm traveling."

Ashley Olsen

Dress-Up—"I love wearing boots under jeans. They look a little dressier than sneakers."

Mischa Barton *(The O.C.)*

Lovin' Layers—"You can never go wrong with sweaters. You can dress them up or down, and they're great for layering."

Fergie

Mix-n-Match—"The way I dress is part of who I am. I don't like wearing just one look. It's important to me that I show my rock 'n' roll and my hip-hop sides with fashion. I don't play by the rules."

Personal Fashion Phobias and Oops!

Anne Hathaway *(Ella Enchanted, Get Smart)*
"Skinny jeans—I love them on other people, but I don't think skinny jeans love me."

Sophia Bush *(One Tree Hill)*
"Acid-wash jeans. But that was ages ago, and we all did them. At least my jeans were in one piece and had no holes in the knees."

Nick Lachey
"When I was 16, I got an embroidered Snoopy sweater from my grandmother. I was a sophomore in high school, trying to be cool, and I got a Snoopy sweater! I returned it the next day."

Usher
"When I look back at photos of myself as a kid, I wonder what my mom was thinking. I'm in those tight little school pants and geeky sweaters. Not so cool, but it wasn't my fault!"

Aly Michalka *(Will)*
"Capris! I don't ever wear them, because I don't feel comfortable [in them]!"

Mandy Moore *(License To Wed)*
"Tube tops! What [is] up with that? They're not very flattering!"

Emma Burton *(Spice Girls)*
"I've fallen over on some platforms and cracked a bone in my ankle, which wasn't very funny."

SELENA GOMEZ
Style

Wizards of Waverly Place's Selena Gomez insists that her fashion style and taste are all about comfort. According to Selena, you can't be comfortable unless you are wearing shoes that feel as if they were made for you!

So, while some Hollywood stars may be into 6-inch heels by Jimmy Choo or Christian Louboutin, Selena is cozy-comfy with her closet full of Converse sneakers!

"When I was just starting out, I went to a lot of auditions," explains Selena. "The other girls' hair was perfect, and they had outfits that were all neat. I came in my own way. My mom had taught me to be myself, and if they don't want that, there's nothing I can do about it….I think you look best when you stand out. The time I got my first pair of Converse is when I realized this is who I'm supposed to be. This is who I am. My Converse [sneakers] were like a calling to me….I got my first pair of black ones, and now I have at least 20 pairs….I'm not really high maintenance. In the morning it takes me five to ten minutes to get ready, especially when I go to work or school. I get up, brush my teeth, put on my sweatpants and Converse, and go!"

Selena Gomez Style Tip
"BE YOURSELF"

Selena's Style

⭐ I like to wear…"Fun stuff! Converse and Vans and funky tops and chunky jewelry."

⭐ My only makeup must-have is… "Carmex Lip Balm. It's cool because it's almost like a lipgloss. It gives you this nice, natural look."

⭐ My favorite pair of Converse are…"The ones Jennifer Stone [her costar] gave me for my birthday. I love the British flag, and she drew the British flag on my green pair of Converse. I love them!"

"DEAR" AMANDA

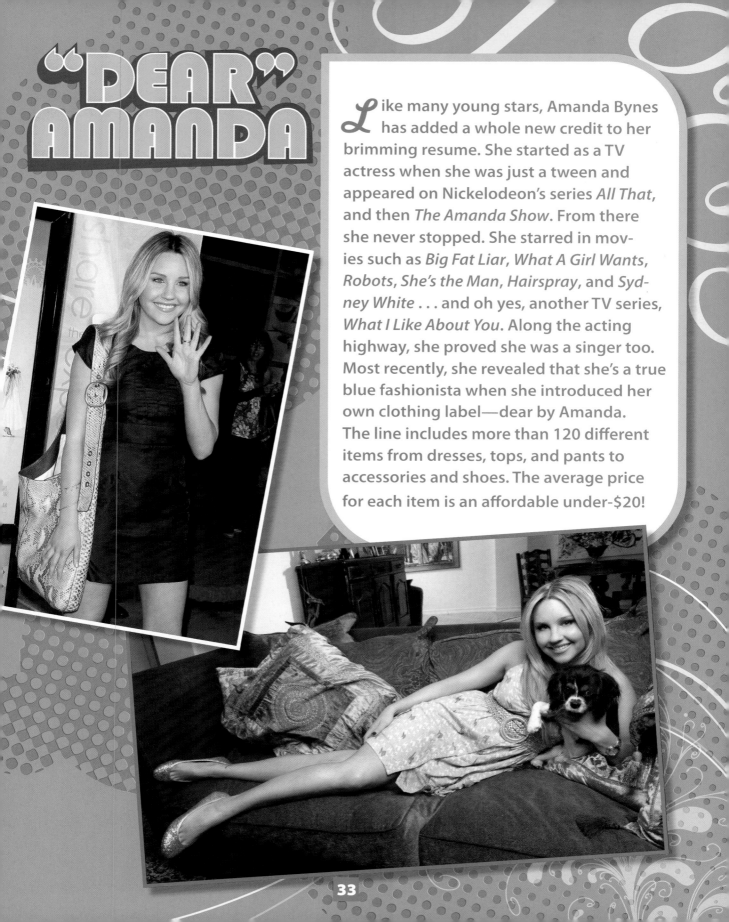

*L*ike many young stars, Amanda Bynes has added a whole new credit to her brimming resume. She started as a TV actress when she was just a tween and appeared on Nickelodeon's series *All That*, and then *The Amanda Show*. From there she never stopped. She starred in movies such as *Big Fat Liar*, *What A Girl Wants*, *Robots*, *She's the Man*, *Hairspray*, and *Sydney White* . . . and oh yes, another TV series, *What I Like About You*. Along the acting highway, she proved she was a singer too. Most recently, she revealed that she's a true blue fashionista when she introduced her own clothing label—dear by Amanda. The line includes more than 120 different items from dresses, tops, and pants to accessories and shoes. The average price for each item is an affordable under-$20!

How would you describe dear by Amanda?

Amanda: Fashionable, affordable, and fun. . . . [Girls will] find comfortable clothes, bright colors, hooded sweatshirts with deer images, lots of cute necklaces and bracelets, cute jeans, unique-looking dresses—different items that have my style. This is my version. No item costs more than $19.98. I didn't want to loan my name to some expensive brand. This makes it really special. It's nice to make it inexpensive for girls in school.

Who inspired the line?

Amanda: I definitely was inspired by my mom. My mom has a very go-getter attitude.

When did you start designing clothes?

Amanda: When I was sixteen, I drew a tank top with an asymmetrical bottom. I knew I would love to make it. So I bought silk, went to a tailor, and had it made. When I was filming *Hairspray*, I got a call from Steve & Barry's saying that they would like me to design a line of clothes for them. I was excited because they didn't even know I had tried to do that on my own. It was a perfect fit for me.

How did you come up with the name "dear"?

Amanda: I collaborate with the women designers for Steve & Barry's. I bring my style-related ideas—what I think is interesting. One of the women brought in a picture of a deer, a black and white silhouette. So it just dawned on me—we could call it "Amanda deer" or "deer," but spell it, d-e-a-r. We all liked it, and they wanted to see if it was trademarked already. It wasn't! So we snagged the name "dear"! I like that it's different. It's hard to come up with a name that hasn't been created yet.

Everything is under $20—why is pricing so important to you?

Amanda: To be affordable for everyone. I look at jeans now, and I can't believe they are $250. It kind of hurts.

Do you have to be a skinny-mini to fit in dear by Amanda outfits?

Amanda: We are definitely doing stuff for all body shapes. We're trying to make fashionable clothes that girls can wear in high school or out to the movies that can make any girl feel cute.

Amanda's Quick Tips

⭐ "I like to mix and match long necklaces and different colors."

✪ "It's important that I feel comfortable."

✪ "I love cool sneakers for fall. You can wear them with skirts or jeans, and they're great when it rains."

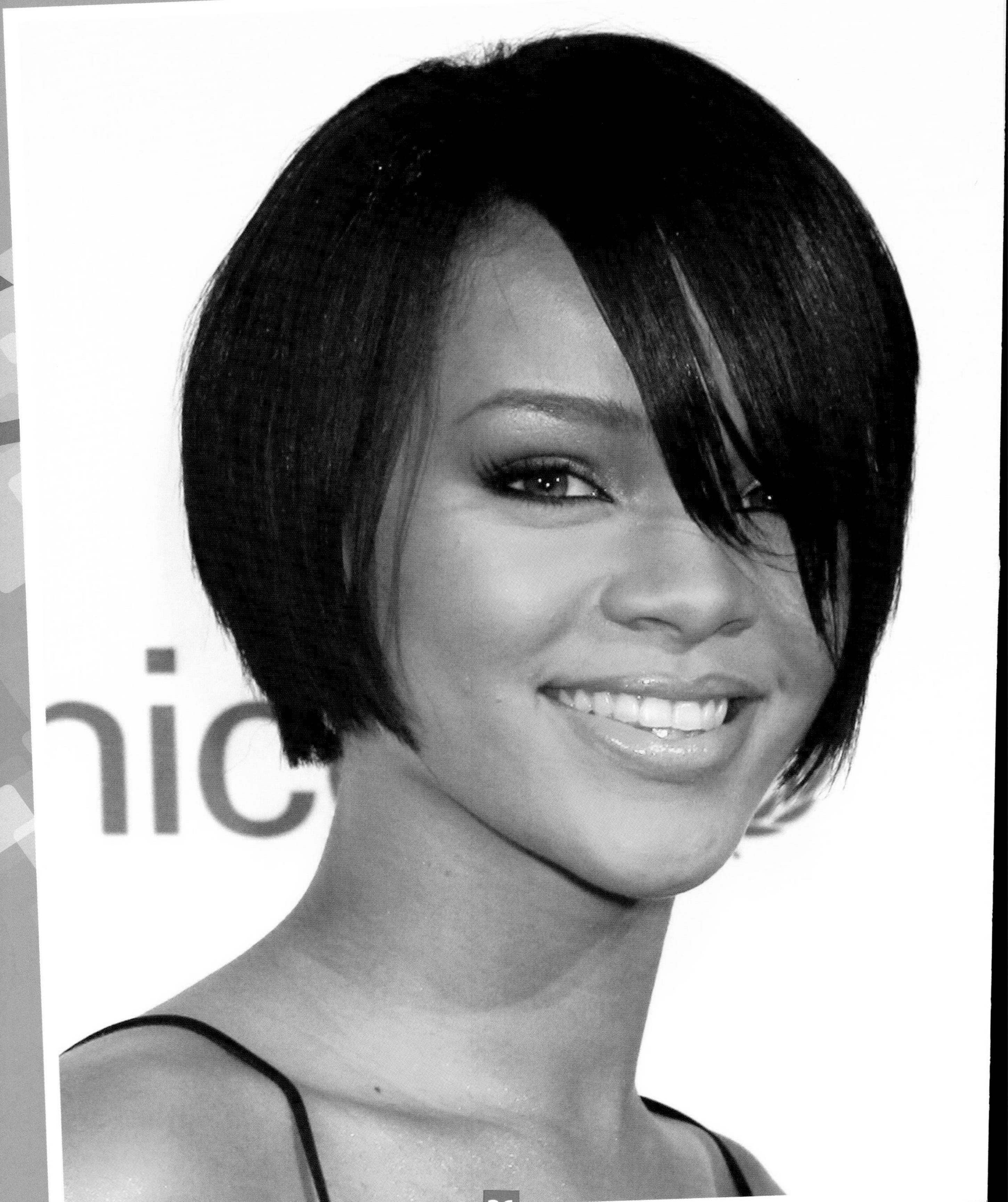

RIHANNA
Island Girl to Diva

Rihanna, the beauty from the tropical isle of Barbados, first exploded onto the music scene in 2005. Since then she has picked up awards from Teen Choice to Grammies, from Billboard to World Music, and many more. She's a multi-platinum diva—there's no question about that. But Rihanna is something else—a style setter. From her long flowing hair to her most recent bob-crop, from her sleek, sophisticated designer side to her let's-have-fun casual look, Rihanna has become a girl to watch!

Diva

1   2   3   4

Rihanna On Fashion

"The most important tip is to always dress to suit you and your personality. You should never try to dress to look like anyone else, because it doesn't always work for you."

"I like to set trends rather than follow."

"In Barbados it's so hot, so it's all about staying hydrated. I drink lots of water and try to keep my skin moisturized."

"I've been a fashion fanatic since I was little . . . looking at all the international magazines. But I used to dress like a boy when I was a kid. I'd wear my brother's baggy pants and his sneakers. Now I like little skullcaps, jeans, flat boots that come up to the knees. And then I play around with the top—a big T-shirt, or a sleek camisole, or a jacket. I love jackets!"

Rihanna's Oops Moment!

"I was four, and my great-grandma was watching us. I used to give her so much trouble. She probably yelled at me, so I went into my mom's room, took her nail polishes, opened them, and painted 'bracelets' up my arm. Then I poured them into a toy hard hat my brother had. When my mom came home, she got really upset. I got scared because I thought, my gosh, I have to go to school like this! Because we never used to have nail-polish remover!"

DIY WITH Emily

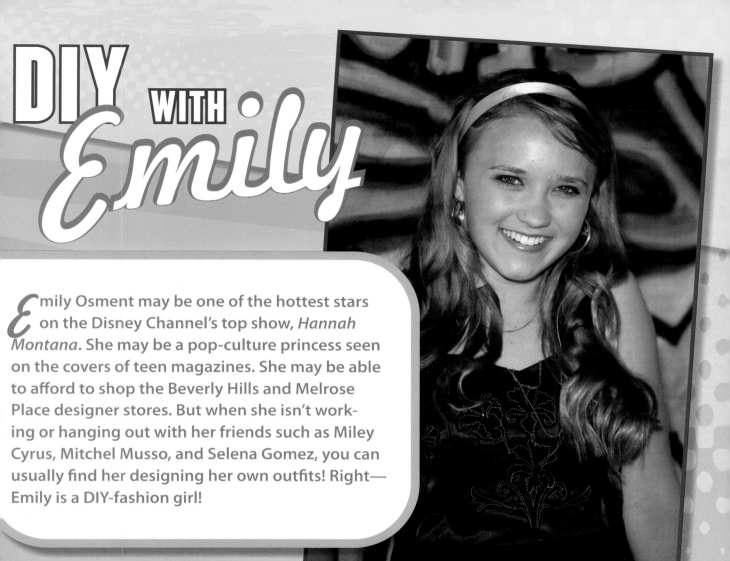

*E*mily Osment may be one of the hottest stars on the Disney Channel's top show, *Hannah Montana*. She may be a pop-culture princess seen on the covers of teen magazines. She may be able to afford to shop the Beverly Hills and Melrose Place designer stores. But when she isn't working or hanging out with her friends such as Miley Cyrus, Mitchel Musso, and Selena Gomez, you can usually find her designing her own outfits! Right—Emily is a DIY-fashion girl!

"I'm really into style," Emily says. "I love to go to my sewing machine and make wacky clothes. People will be like, 'Wow, that's new!' and I'm like, 'Yeah.' I'm not afraid. The polka-dot dress I wore in a [recent photo shoot], I made right before school a while ago. I wore it for my first day. My mom and I really love to sew together. I designed the pattern for the dress I wore to Radio Disney's 10th birthday concert. My mom took my drawing and made it. Sometimes I like to be preppy. And sometimes I like to look fancy and pretty. I have a ton of pink in my closet, but the funny thing is that I normally don't wear pink. I make clothes for friends. It's pretty fun, but I'm a perfectionist. I want all the seams to be straight! My friend, *Read It and Weep*'s Kay Panabaker, and I have been making stuff like shirts and necklaces. When I'm older, I'd like to open a business."

Emily's Fave Stores
★ Forever 21
★ Urban Outfitters
★ American Eagle

Lilly vs. Emily

"I'm not like [my character] Lilly. She has the coolest clothes I have ever seen. I would love to have those kinds of clothes!"

Raiding Closets

"Talk to your friends who wear your same size, [and trade off]. Miley and I share clothes all the time."

Fashion Philosophy

"I like to match. On the show, though, they find colors that look good together that don't match. I'm learning."

Emily's DIY Advice

"I make my own clothes sometimes. I'll put a patch on an old skirt and make it bigger. All fashions come back around."

Stylin'

"My look changes every day. I'm not stuck with some-one saying, 'I know exactly what she's going to wear tomorrow.' I might be preppy, punk, I might be girly."

HAYDEN *Panettiere*

"*I*'ve only recently been able to try out a bunch of different styles without feeling like I'm dressing beyond my age," says the 18-year-old *Heroes* star. "On the show, I spend most of my time in a cheerleading uniform, so in real life I like to have a lot more fun with my clothes."

Have Fun With Hayden!

⭐ "I'm short, so I'm always on the hunt for cute shoes with a little extra height."

⭐ "I really try to go for it when it comes to color: bright, exotic, greenish-blue might be my favorite."

⭐ Hold back your hair? Headbands are Hayden's solution.

⭐ Skincare—Neutrogena Deep Clean Cream Cleanser. "Because of the show, I'm always putting makeup on, taking it off, and putting it back on again. If I didn't have this cleanser, I think I'd be breaking out all the time."

⭐ More skincare! "Facials are my biggest beauty indulgence. I'm obsessive about my skin."

Clothes For A Cause

Hayden is a big supporter of the Save the Whales! organization. In 2008, Hayden lent her name to their campaign to stop hunters from killing baby seals for their pelts for fur coats and clothes. "Come be a hero and take a stand with me," Hayden wrote on her Web site. "These beautiful animals are not only gentle, but are killed in the most inhumane way. They cannot speak for themselves or beg for mercy, but WE can be their voices for them! It's time to put our foot down. Let's save the seals."

Hayden actually opened her own closet to support this cause.

She offered some of her own personal clothes for auction to raise money to save the seals. Many of them were never-worn designer clothes, donated by major designers to help Hayden's cause.

DESIGNING *Divas*

Ashlee Simpson

Clothing Line: A collection of T-shirts for Wet Seal

Quote: "I was inspired by so many fun, wonderful things as I was recording [her new CD] *Bittersweet World*, and it's been great to carry through those inspirations into these new shirt designs. . . . I hope my fans love this album and rock out in these shirts. . . . I always have my fans in mind. My style shows through, and I think they will appreciate that."

Heidi Montage

Clothing Line: Heidiwood for Anchor Blue

Quote: "I'm obsessed with . . . zebra print. When I was doing my line, I was doing things that inspired me and things that I wished I could find in clothes. So I was like, I love zebra print. There's not enough out there, and so I really wanted to incorporate that in little details."

Lauren Conrad

Clothing Line: Lauren Conrad Collection

Quote: "It's for a girl who has a busy life and needs a wardrobe that goes along with it."

Pete Wentz

Clothing Line: Clandestine Industries by Pete Wentz (limited-edition graphic T-shirts, skinny jeans, and hoodies)

Quote: "My ideas come from my head and my heart. It's not about using my name or my status. . . . [Expect] interesting cuts and design that are a little out of the box."

Avril Lavigne

Clothing Line: Abbey Dawn

Quote: "I have a particular style. I want it to be available to a lot of girls and I want it to be affordable. . . . I actually am the designer. What's really important to me is that everything fits well and is well-made, so I try everything on and approve it all."

Rihanna

Label/Store: Totes and H&M—Rihanna designed a line of umbrellas for Totes and a T-shirt for the Fashion against AIDS collection at H&M

Quote: "I like to be edgy."

Jessica Simpson

Clothing Lines: Princy (original clothing line); JS by Jessica Simpson, Jessica Simpson Footwear, Sweet Kisses (Jessica's lines include clothing, shoes, eyewear, handbags, and fragrance)

Quote: "I am every girl. I want my clothing to be accessible and fun. . . . I want women and girls to feel comfortable and confident wearing my products."

Joel and Benji Madden

Clothing Line: DCMA

Quotes: "We're going to carry DCMA's line [in the new store DCMA Collective]. Baby stuff, the jewelry—it's my favorite—and the collaboration T-shirts."—Joel

"We come from a small town, and not very much, and to be doing this—it's definitely a dream come true."—Benji

Beyoncé

Clothing Line: House of Dereon

Quote: "People my age love fashion and want to dress in designer clothes, but can't afford it. I want to do something that is affordable, but sophisticated and feminine—something I would wear."

Hilary Duff

Clothing Line: Stuff by Hilary Duff (Styles include clothes, accessories, and fragrance "With Love . . . Hilary Duff")

Quote: "I love clothes. I can't control myself. I [adore] shoes and clothes and makeup. I'm the kind of person who doesn't like to wear things over and over again."

Will.I.Am

Clothing Line: i.am.

Quote: "I started making people jackets, then hoodies, then sweaters, and I got them into stores."

Sean "Diddy" Combs

Clothing Line: Sean John (Suits, shirts, jeans, T-shirts, fragrance)

Quote: "I'm constantly trying to evolve and grow."